Explaining The Euro
To A Washington Audience

Tommaso Padoa-Schioppa

Published by
Group of Thirty©
Washington, DC
2001

Contents

I. Introduction

The introduction of the euro and the establishment of the European Central Bank (ECB) mark the virtual completion of the process of European integration in the economic and monetary field. At the same time, it opens an entirely new chapter, and poses new challenges, in this same process.

The purpose of this Lecture is to explain the above to an audience, whose multiple interests reflect the many facets of the city of Washington. This is indeed the city where the two Bretton Woods' sister institutions have their seat, the Federal Reserve System has its headquarters, and a federally constituted State has its capital. Being the capital of the greatest world power, Washington is also the city that influences international relations most. By taking these four points of view in succession, I shall try to illustrate how the ECB works and what challenges it faces as a result of the fact that the European Union, contrary to the US, is far from being a full political union.

II. From Bretton Woods To Maastricht

The Treaty of Rome, signed in 1957, set the objective of creating a "common market" among six European countries. The concept of the common market was formulated as the so-called "four freedoms" of circulation for goods, persons, services and capital among these countries. An institutional structure was created to establish the common market and to provide its governance.

Implicit in the Treaty of Rome is the proposition that the order of a common market requires a corresponding monetary order. This proposition is only implicit because, in the mid-fifties, such monetary order—the system of fixed exchange rates designed at Bretton Woods in 1944—was firmly in place and seen as almost ever lasting at the world level. As it provided an adequate anchor to monetary stability also to a region such as Europe, debates about what kind of monetary arrangement should complement the common market only started when the Bretton Woods system began to show signs of weakness, i.e. in the mid sixties.

The eventual collapse of the dollar-based system (1973) was followed by a period of about fifteen years in which the attempt to ensure exchange rate stability at the European level used the Deutsche mark as the anchor currency. The first of such attempts was the "Snake" of 1973. In 1979 the Snake was replaced by the European Monetary System (EMS), which underwent various phases and reforms over the years and was hit by a serious crisis in 1992-93.

Until the mid-eighties the program of fully establishing the four freedoms had been largely implemented for goods, much less for services, and even less for capital and persons. The whole program gained new impetus in the second half of the eighties and was virtually achieved in 1993.

Both the collapse of the Bretton Woods system in 1973 and the 1992-1993 EMS crisis illustrate that open trade and free capital mobility makes fixed exchange rates eventually incompatible with independent monetary policies. The four elements form an "inconsistent quartet". The 1973 decision to drop the exchange rate element and move to a regime of floating rates was one way to overcome the inconsistency. Another way was the 1992 stipulation of the Maastricht Treaty, whereby Europe decided to drop independent national monetary policies and adopt a single currency to complement the Single Market. Unlike the Bretton Woods adjustable peg and the EMS, EMU is *not* a binding *international* exchange rate arrangement. Instead, it establishes at the European level the *domestic* monetary order that normally exists within a nation: *one* currency, *one* central bank, *one* monetary policy.

III. Two Central Banks

"Eurosystem" is the word chosen by the ECB to indicate the "ECB plus the participating central banks", of which there are twelve today. The Eurosystem is the central bank of the euro just as the Federal Reserve System is the central bank of the dollar. It is therefore natural to compare the structure and competencies of these two institutions.

Like the Federal Reserve System, the Eurosystem has no legal personality. The ECB Statute indicates that the Eurosystem "shall be governed by the decision-making bodies of the ECB". These are the Governing Council and the Executive Board, both chaired by the President of the ECB.

The Governing Council is composed of the six members of the Executive Board and the governors of the national central banks, who sit in a personal capacity, not as representatives of their countries or institutions. The key task of the Governing Council is to "formulate the monetary policy of the Community" and to "establish the necessary guidelines" for its implementation.

The Executive Board of the ECB consists of the President, the Vice-President and four other members. They are appointed for a period of eight years by the Heads of States or Government, on a recommendation from the EU Council of Ministers, after the European Parliament has been consulted. The Executive Board "shall implement monetary policy in accordance with guidelines and decisions laid down by the Governing Council. In doing so, the Executive Board shall give the necessary instructions to national central banks." The Executive Board also prepares the meetings of the Governing Council and manages the day-to-day business of the ECB.

As the Fed in the US, so in Europe the Eurosystem belongs to the level of the "federation". In both cases monetary policy decisions are fully centralised, at the level of the Governing Council and the Federal Open Market Committee, respectively, thus reflecting the indivisible character of monetary policy. The fact that the operations of the Eurosystem are carried out—to the extent possible and appropriate—by the participating national central banks, does not contradict the federal profile of the institution.

Although a federal and decentralised central bank is not a novelty, the Eurosystem is a special case. First, in contrast with the Fed's District Banks that were uniformly created with the same legislative act that generated the Federal Reserve System, the national central banks of the Eurosystem are old institutions with diverse traditions and statutes. They have for many generations and until the introduction of the euro performed the full range of central banking functions under their own responsibility. They have been accountable to, and sometimes dependent on, national institutions. Public opinion has perceived, and still perceives, them as national institutions. Their tasks, organisations, statutes and cultures preserve clear differences. All this makes it much less natural for the national central banks to become parts of the Eurosystem than it was for the US District Banks with the Fed's System.

Second, while New York was already the key financial centre and market in the US when the Federal Reserve System was created, in the euro area each country hosts its own banking system, one (or more) financial centres, and national financial markets. A consequence of this difference is that, compared with the Fed, the implementation of monetary policy in the Eurosystem is more strongly directed from the centre and less centralised in its execution. The Fed operates through the New York Fed, the Eurosystem through all NCBs, and even if the pound joined the euro, London would not play the role that New York plays in the Federal Reserve System.

Third, the fields of competence differ in the Fed and the Eurosystem. Central banking is composed of monetary policy, the oversight of payment systems and banking supervision. In the US the totality of this triadic function is entrusted to the Federal

Reserve System, though not in an exclusive way for banking supervision. In the euro area, banking supervision remains a national competence, entrusted in most cases to the national central bank, but not to the Eurosystem. The competence of the ECB in this area is mainly consultative.

Finally, the Eurosystem and the Federal Reserve System have different communication practices. The ECB President holds extended press conferences once a month after a Governing Council meeting, at which he delivers a comprehensive introductory statement which explains the decisions taken and outlines in detail the reasoning and the main arguments which have led to the decision. A question and answer session allows the media and the public to gain further insights into the deliberations of the Governing Council. Both the introductory statement and the question and answer session are made available on the ECB web-site before the end of the day. By contrast, the Federal Reserve System issues a brief statement regarding the monetary policy decisions immediately after each meeting, while the underlying reasoning and the arguments that have led to the decisions can be found six weeks later in the minutes of the meetings of the Federal Open Market Committee.

It is interesting to compare the United States and the euro area also with respect to the way in which monetary policy interacts with the other key economic policies: budget, employment and structural policies.

While in the United States both monetary and fiscal policies are conducted at the federal level, in Europe only monetary policy is "federal". In the fiscal field the so-called Stability and Growth Pact provides overall discipline by setting binding constraints to the size of budget deficit in each individual Member State. It does not, however, permit the prior definition of a fiscal stance for the EU because budgetary decisions are the preserve of the Member States. Employment too remains predominantly a competence of Member states, with labour legislation and contracts mainly stipulated at the national level.

To this unique European institutional setting three main criticisms have been expressed by prominent US academics. None of them can be rejected altogether, since each points to problems that actually exist. Yet there are important counter arguments that need to be taken into account.

The first criticism, made by Prof. Dornbusch, concerns *labour mobility*. To be optimal, a currency area needs a high degree of factor mobility that Europe does not have in the field of labour. To this argument it can be answered that not only in Europe as a whole, but also in individual European countries there is a lack of labour mobility, which is due to cultural and societal factors as much as to economic ones. Italy, for instance, has a rate of unemployment of around 20 per cent in the South and 4 per cent in the North. In spite of this, people are reluctant to move from South to North. A similar situation occurs in Germany with its East-West dualism. The lack of labour mobility is not euro-area specific, but rather country specific.

The second criticism, made by Prof. Krugman, concerns *asymmetric shocks*. Since the advent of the euro, the possibility has been eliminated to modify the exchange rate, perhaps the most effective instrument to respond to shocks that hit one country only. However, the resulting loss in policy efficiency is much more limited than the argument suggests. Not all, indeed few, asymmetric shocks are country specific. More often they are sector, or industry, or region specific, so that their boundaries do not coincide with national boundaries. For instance, when the steel industry underwent a crisis in the seventies the large region heavily hit was located across France, Luxembourg, Belgium, and Germany, and policy responses needed to be directed from Brussels and could not be monetary anyway. Moreover, when looking carefully, one realises that most of the asymmetric shocks that are country-specific are in fact policy induced. With monetary union and the constraints that now limit fiscal policies at the national level, asymmetric shocks can no longer come from monetary or fiscal policy. As far as asymmetric shocks are concerned, the advent of the single currency actually represents an improvement compared to the previous situation.

The third criticism, made by Prof. Feldstein, concerns *national conflicts*. Europe would be too diverse and heterogeneous, and the role of the nation state still too relevant, for a smooth decision-making in bodies like the ECB, or the EU Council of ministers, to be smooth and peaceful. Conflict, rather than progress towards closer union, will be the result of this state of affairs. My counter argument is that there is no indication that this danger is materialising. The ECB takes its decisions by adopting a euro area-wide approach that considers not the situation in individual countries, but that of the euro area as a whole. Members of the ECB Governing Council are not (and do not regard themselves) as national representatives negotiating to achieve the most favourable result for their own country. They are eighteen individuals who try to reach the optimal collective decision for the whole euro area. It should not be forgotten, after all, that European integration is a *remedy* to previous, and much worse, conflicts, not a *recipe* for new ones.

Yet, even taking the counter arguments into account, one should recognise that the problems raised by the critics do exist. If, for example, wages and salaries in one country were put out of line by a national agreement, the resulting divergence and loss of competitiveness could no longer be cured, as so many times in the past, with the exchange rate. And even though the US themselves did not have a macro-economically significant federal budget until about sixty years ago, it remains that the lack of a European fiscal policy may be a serious shortcoming in certain circumstances. Over time, these weaknesses will have to be tackled and corrected. I would submit, however, that corrective action must address the incompleteness of the European constitutional setting and the occasionally inconsistent behaviour of economic agents, rather than the part of the edifice built so far.

IV. Two Constitutions

Let me now turn to that part of the Washington audience for which the most interesting comparison between the US and the EU concerns constitutional matters. Trying to understand such matters is necessary for politicians and citizens, but also for central bankers, because no important public function—and the management of the currency is undoubtedly one—can be adequately performed if it is not cast in the appropriate constitutional framework. To fully understand the working of the ECB it is therefore important to analyse how the constitution of the EU compares with the US one.

There are three main similarities between the constitutional framework in the EU and US. First, both the EU and the US rely on written constitutions, the Rome-Maastricht Treaty and the Constitution issued by the Philadelphia convention of 1787, respectively. Second, both these charters were the outcome of free and democratic political processes, not of a concession on the part of a sovereign. Third, both substantiate the term "Union" insofar as they indicate how certain powers are allocated above the state level.

Between the two constitutions there are, however, also obvious and fundamental differences. Two stand out prominently. The first is that the Rome-Maastricht Treaty has mainly an economic content, whereas the only relevant economic article in the US Constitution deals with interstate commerce. When the US Constitution was drafted, the involvement of the state in economic matters was very limited indeed. The total size of the budget, as well as its share in the national income, were quite small and there was no central bank. In the US a central bank was created more than a hundred years after the adoption of the federal Constitution. By contrast, the process of forming the European Union took economic activity as its starting point and predominant field, and it did so at a historical juncture in which the state had already accumulated considerable, possibly excessive, powers in the economic sphere.

The second and more fundamental difference is that, unlike the US, Europe has only a partial political union. Indeed, the already existing elements of a political union in Europe do not suffice to form a full political union. They are however very important and often overlooked by outside observers, who easily liken the EU to loose regional arrangements such as Mercosur or Asean. So let me briefly review them before stressing the differences between the EU and the US.

- The first existing element of a political union is that the EU has by now full competence for the economic, monetary and financial field. The legislation concerning products and markets mainly originates from Brussels. Competition policy is a prerogative of the European Commission. Budgetary decisions, albeit national, are subject to the rule of the Stability and Growth Pact, while in the US there is no federal rule for the State budgets. There is a single currency and a single monetary policy that, like other decisions fields of central banking, are the responsibility of the ECB. If all these matters had previously constituted a major portion in the exercise of political power in EU Member States, how can it be denied that the European Union, to which these functions are now assigned, is indeed a political construct?

- The second element is that the establishment of the four freedoms has required the setting up a state-like institutional system, with legislative and executive capacity, an elected parliament, and judiciary functions. In this respect the EU is completely different from any so-called international organisation, and much closer to the US institutional system.

- The third element is that, to establish, maintain and regulate the four freedoms, the EU has gone a long way in exerting power in fields that transcend the purely economic field, like immigration, human rights, health protection, cultural or environmental issues. The simple reason is that economic and non-economic aspects of life are hardly separable.

These important features, however, while necessary, are not sufficient to identify the EU as a political union. In both the competencies and the institutions key elements are missing.

As for the *competencies*, the EU still lacks those that have been the historical *raison d'être* of the state: first and foremost the provision of internal and external security to the people. The steps taken in Maastricht, Amsterdam and Nice towards the development of a European foreign and security policy, as well as in internal affairs, are just a beginning that remains very far from filling the gap.

As for the *institutions*, the EU is still not complying with the key principles that form the heritage of western constitutionalism. First and foremost, the majority principle is far from being fully applied. The EU not only, unlike any unitary state, lacks the generalised adoption of the majority principle in all fields of potential common decision. It also bears the fundamental contradiction of combining recognised competencies with the requirement that related decisions should be unanimous. It is not an exaggeration to say that a true union begins where the rule of unanimity ends. Indeed unanimity makes it impossible to pursue any meaningful notion of *general* interest, it only permits to act when *particular* interests coincide or in the very rare occasions in which all parties happen to share the same view of what the general interest requires in the case in point. Moreover, the extent to which power in the EU is rooted in the popular vote still falls short of the requirement of modern democratic constitutions. It is possible, for example, to adopt legislation without a positive vote of the European Parliament. Finally, the powers of the various institutions of the Union have not yet reached a satisfactory equilibrium.

Neither the US Fed nor any other central bank in the world is, like the Eurosystem, confronted with the challenge of *not* being the expression of a political union. This is indeed a challenge, because normally the soundness of a currency does not rest exclusively on the central bank. It derives from a multiplicity of elements that only a state or, more broadly, a political union provides. When we say, for example, that a currency is a "safe haven" we refer not only to the quality and credibility of its central bank, but also to the solidity of the whole social, political and economic structure to which it belongs. Historical experience shows that if that structure appears to weaken, also the currency weakens, irrespective of the actions of the central bank. A strong currency requires a strong economy and a strong polity, not only a competent central bank. The central bank is, and should remain, an institution with too limited a mission to replace the lack of a political union.

The problems posed by the coexistence of a single currency with a still unachieved political union will influence European developments in the coming years. They will have implications both for the Eurosystem and for politicians. The *Eurosystem* will have to be aware of the special difficulties and responsibilities deriving from this anomalous condition. It will have to cope with this situation and adapt its attitudes to a composite—EU and national—institutional architecture. It will also have to be prepared for the further evolution of that same architecture. For *politicians* the implication is that they should not forget the commitment that was implicit in their decision to move ahead with monetary union in advance of political union.

V. International Relations

Today Washington D.C. is the most important political centre in the world. In Europe, there have been several cities—like Athens, Rome, Paris, Vienna and London—that have had at some stage of their history an equally important influence on international affairs.

Hence the fourth aspect of this Lecture, which stems from the following question: What is the significance of the euro for international relations? Let me state at the outset that the introduction of the euro is unlikely, in my view, to affect the present state of *floating exchange rates* between the three main currencies. It is indeed widely agreed today that a system of more or less fixed exchange rates is neither feasible nor desirable at the global level. The reason is that the major players cannot be realistically expected, in the foreseeable future, to achieve the high degree of co-ordination and political commitment that would be required for such system to function, i.e. to overcome the contradiction embedded in the "inconsistent quartet". Floating exchange rates among the major currencies are bound to stay.

That said, the advent of the euro in an increasingly interdependent world is a major event at least under four economic, political and institutional respects that are especially relevant to this audience, precisely because the US is the leading power in today's world.

- First, the euro is likely to grow in an *anchor role* for third country currencies. While none of the three key currencies is likely to submit its monetary policy to the constraint of an exchange rate commitment in the foreseeable future, other countries will attempt to escape the instability associated with floating and look for an external monetary anchor. For economies that are small and open relative to the US and the EU, the natural anchor will be the currency of the economy with which trade and financial relationships are closest. Already now, the monetary or exchange rate regime of a significant number of Central and Eastern European and African countries involves the euro in an exclusive or partial role.

  The present arrangements are mainly a legacy of past links to the former national currencies of the euro area countries. In the future, the euro could gain further importance as a reference currency for the more than eighty countries located in what could be called the European hemisphere, i.e. the European, Mediterranean and African region. The twelve countries that are now negotiating their accession to the EU represent a prominent case, because their efforts to achieve economic and financial integration with the EU will require special attention to the exchange rate. As to other countries in the European hemisphere, for virtually all of them the EU is by far the largest trading partner, the base of their financial system and a counterpart in important bilateral agreements in the fields of trade, technical assistance and support for economic development. It is uncertain whether the dollar and the yen will extend their role as an anchor for the monetary policy of countries in the American hemisphere and in the East Asia and Pacific region to the extent the euro will probably do in the European hemisphere.

- Second, the EU and the euro seems to indicate the importance of *regional arrangements* as an integral part of the system of world governance. The European Union is a successful example of how international co-operation in certain fields can be organised on a regional scale without endangering the multilateral character of the overall system of international relations, but rather complementing and strengthening it. Attempts to promote the regional dimension of international co-operation are being made in other parts of the world, in particular the Western Hemisphere. NAFTA and Mercosur indeed aim at a free-trade area and a custom union in the Northern and in the Southern part, respectively, of that hemisphere. However, with the establishment of the single market and of the single currency, Europe has gone much farther. The European experience shows that a degree of regionalism in organising relations between countries is a precious intermediate layer in a world where the number of sovereign countries has grown to almost two hundreds.

- Third, the introduction of the euro modifies the present *international configuration* of institutions and fora. By reducing to three the number of relevant players, the advent of the euro *simplifies* and makes the process of co-operation more efficient, possibly facilitating the formulation of common understandings. It is true that no G3 has come into being as yet as a result of the euro, nor is this likely to come in the near future. However, the debates within the G7 have rapidly evolved from a round table of seven countries to a focused discussion on the three major economies, their situations, how they interact and the implications for the rest of the world. From the point of view of the bilateral relationships between Europe and the US, this contributes to achieving a more balanced situation.

But the euro also *complicates* international co-operation. The euro corresponds to a regional entity formed by several largely sovereign states. From an *economic* policy point of view, this peculiarity complicates the co-operative game because it introduces a player, who conducts different policies (monetary, fiscal, structural) at different levels (European, national, sub-national). While Japan and the United States are, to a very large extent, single-tier entities, Europe is a multi-tier one. From an *institutional* point of view, the complication stems from the fact that all international organisations and fora are built on the presumption that their members are countries and that policy responsibility rests with the country. A full accommodation of the Eurosystem in organisations such as the IMF, the BIS, the G7 or the OECD would require rather difficult adjustments, because the euro area is neither a country nor a single-tier policy-maker. In the present international institutional framework, both the Eurosystem and the EU still have a somewhat special position, because they cannot claim the status of full members. At the same time, the countries that have adopted the euro have also changed their positions, because they are no longer responsible for one of the key policies that form the object of international co-operation. Furthermore, in fora such as the G7 or the G10 the Eurosystem also speaks on behalf of numerous countries (eight for the G7, six for the G10) that are not members of those same fora. For procedures involving consultation and the circulation of information, this is clearly a complication.

- The fourth element concerns the conjugation of economic *integration and governance*. This is something that the process of European integration has succeeded in a much more balanced and effective way than the process of globalisation. Compared to globalisation, Europe constitutes a much more innovative and a far-reaching model of international relations.

Notoriously, the market system is a legal, social, and institutional order, not only an economic one. That it needs a strong set of public arrangements to function effectively is considered obvious at the national, or domestic, level, while it is often forgotten or even denied at the international level.

Now, the European experience is one in which the various elements that compose the market system have been developed jointly, in a rather balanced way. The legal and institutional infrastructure, which normally exists for a national market economy, has been built for the European Community through the institutions created by the Treaty of Rome. This has entailed common legislation and regulations, law enforcement mechanisms, decision-making capacities and majority voting rules. It is noteworthy, for example, that only by broadening the scope of majority voting and establishing a closer link between this rule-making function and the democratic process, the Single Market could finally be achieved. Examples are provided in many fields: banking, the liberalisation of the market for public utilities, competition policy, etc.

Moreover, policy cannot rely exclusively on rules and there is, and there must always be room for discretion. We know perfectly well that, within a single state, institutions are an indispensable means to organise human relations largely because of the unavoidable room for discretion in the interpretation or implementation of rules. All this tends, again, to be forgotten and denied when we come to the field of international relations.

While state policy systems have often suffered from an excess of discretion and have gradually moved towards a more rule-based approach, at the international level the possibility of discretionary action is still rare and grossly insufficient. This essentially derives from the lack of institutions entrusted with the exercise of discretionary power, which, in turn, is due to a reluctance to shift sovereignty above the nation state.

Again, if we look at the European experience, we see a significant example of institution building and of the exercise discretion. Europe has created a capacity to cope with the phenomenon of internationalisation that has not been achieved to a comparable degree at the global level. Only the future will show whether the European experience can find its way into the institutional profile of global institutions.

In the present state of the world, the preservation of economic order requires countries to be conscious of their international responsibilities. This is a matter of both enlightened self-interest and international public spirit. Indeed, where countries or regions are economically and financially interdependent there are, as in any integrated economy, certain public goods, which are "public" with respect to a group of countries, a continent, or the world itself. Global financial stability and the maintenance of open trade are prominent examples. Such international public goods cannot be expected to automatically result from the spontaneous behaviour of market participants and national governments, for the same reason for which, within an economy, public goods are not produced by the market. Spontaneous behaviour tends to ignore the numerous externalities that arise at the international level. International institutions and fora exist to address these externalities and, indeed, they try to. In general, the European experience shows that a degree of supra-nationalism can be a sine qua non condition for an effective provision of international public goods, just as a national power is indispensable for the provision of national public goods.

VI. Conclusions

This Lecture has taken the point of view of four components of a Washington audience to illustrate the challenges raised by the advent of the euro. But there is also a fifth component of this audience, the academic community, which needs to be mentioned.

Many of the issues I have discussed have no straightforward solution because the EU is an unprecedented experiment in political, social and economic engineering. This was also the case when the United States of America were created as a federal state. The US was probably the first example of a society trying to achieve a clear consensus on which powers are to be exercised at the centre and which powers should be exercised at the periphery. That consensus has been the most distinctive feature and the very basis of US democracy. A similar process is still ongoing in the EU, where consensus on this crucial issue has been achieved only in limited areas.

From an intellectual point of view, federalism is a fascinating subject because it relates to the definition of the area, in which a good is in fact public, i.e. whether it is a local public good or whether, at the other extreme, it is a world one. Not all public goods are public in the same sense. If, ultimately, the essence of a policy function in the economy is to pursue a public good or a public interest; and if it is true that "public" may mean different things for different communities; and if the optimum is to be neither below nor above the level at which a good needs to be recognised as public, then a multi-tier governance of the economy is necessary.

In shaping a consensus on these issues in the US, the contribution of men of knowledge was at least as important as the one given by politicians. This should also be the case in Europe, since the issues raised by the advent of the European Union represent an intellectual, and not only political, challenge. Both sides of the Atlantic are involved in this challenge. One should not forget how deep was the influence of European political thought on men like Jay, Madison, Hamilton and Franklin. Cross-fertilisation between Europe and the US should resume if we want a successful completion of the European integration process.

Group of Thirty Members

Sr. Guillermo de la Dehesa
Consejero Delegado
Banco Pastor

Professor Gerhard Fels
Director
Institut der deutschen Wirtschaft

Mr. Stanley Fischer
Principal Deputy Managing Director
International Monetary Fund

Mr. Arminio Fraga Neto
Governor
Banco Central do Brasil

Mr. Toyoo Gyohten
Senior Advisor, The Bank of Tokyo-Mitsubishi, Ltd.
President, Institute for International Monetary Affairs

Mr. Gerd Hausler
Counsellor and Director, International Capital Markets Department
International Monetary Fund

Mr. John G. Heimann
Senior Advisor, Merrill Lynch & Co., Inc.

Professor Peter B. Kenen
Walker Professor of Economics & International Finance,
Department of Economics, Princeton University

Mr. Mervyn King
Deputy Governor
Bank of England

Professor Paul Krugman
Professor of Economics
Woodrow Wilson School, Princeton University

M. Jacques de Larosière
Conseiller
BNP Paribas

Mr. William McDonough
President
Federal Reserve Bank of New York

Mr. Shijuro Ogata
Former Deputy Governor
Bank of Japan

Mr. Guillermo Ortiz Martinez
Governor
Banco de Mexico

Dr. Sylvia Ostry
Distinguished Research Fellow
Munk Centre for International Studies, Toronto

Dr. Tommaso Padoa-Schioppa
Member of the Executive Board
European Central Bank

Group of Thirty Publications

Reports:

Reducing the Risks of International Insolvency
A Compendium of Work in Progress. 2000

Collapse: The Venezuelan Banking Crisis of '94
Ruth de Krivoy. 2000

**The Evolving Corporation: Global Imperatives
and National Responses**
Study Group Report. 1999

International Insolvencies in the Financial Sector
Study Group Report. 1998

Global Institutions, National Supervision and Systemic Risk
Study Group on Supervision and Regulation. 1997

Latin American Capital Flows: Living with Volatility
Latin American Capital Flows Study Group. 1994

**Defining the Roles of Accountants, Bankers and
Regulators in the United States**
Study Group on Accountants, Bankers and Regulators. 1994

EMU After Maastricht
Peter B. Kenen. 1992

Sea Changes in Latin America
Pedro Aspe, Andres Bianchi and Domingo Cavallo, with discussion by
S.T. Beza and William Rhodes. 1992

The Summit Process and Collective Security:
Future Responsibility Sharing
The Summit Reform Study Group. 1991

Financing Eastern Europe
Richard A. Debs, Harvey Shapiro and Charles Taylor. 1991

The Risks Facing the World Economy
The Risks Facing the World Economy Study Group. 1991

The William Taylor Memorial Lectures

Post Crisis Asia: The Way Forward
Lee Hsien Loong. 2001

Licensing Banks: Still Necessary?
Tommaso Padoa-Schioppa. 2000

Banking Supervision and Financial Stability
Andrew Crockett. 1998

Global Risk Management
Ulrich Cartellieri and Alan Greenspan. 1996

The Financial Disruptions of the 1980s:
A Central Banker Looks Back
E. Gerald Corrigan. 1993

Special Reports:

Derivatives: Practices and Principles: Follow-up
Surveys of Industry Practice
Global Derivatives Study Group. 1994

Derivatives: Practices and Principles, Appendix III:
Survey of Industry Practice
Global Derivatives Study Group. 1994

Derivatives: Practices and Principles, Appendix II:
Legal Enforceability: Survey of Nine Jurisdictions
Global Derivatives Study Group. 1993

Derivatives: Practices and Principles, Appendix I:
Working Papers
Global Derivatives Study Group. 1993

Derivatives: Practices and Principles
Global Derivatives Study Group. 1993

Clearance and Settlement Systems: Status Reports,
Autumn 1992
Various Authors. 1992

Clearance and Settlement Systems: Status Reports,
Year-End 1990
Various Authors. 1991

Conference on Clearance and Settlement Systems;
London, March 1990: Speeches
Various Authors. 1990

Clearance and Settlement Systems: Status Reports,
Spring 1990
Various Authors. 1990

Clearance and Settlement Systems in the World's
Securities Markets
*Steering & Working Committees of the Securities Clearance and
Settlement Study. 1988*

Occasional Papers:

63. Exchange Rate Regimes: Some Lessons from
Postwar Europe
Charles Wyplosz. 2000

62. Decisionmaking for European Economic and
Monetary Union
Erik Hoffmeyer. 2000

61. Charting a Course for the Multilateral Trading System:
The Seattle Ministerial Meeting and Beyond
Ernest H. Preeg. 1999

60. Exchange Rate Arrangements for Emerging
Market Economies
Felipe Larraín and Andrés Velasco. 1999